To Callum
On your third birthday
Love From Zac and Sarah
      x   x

Over on the Farm

A counting picture book rhyme

For N.G.

TRANSWORLD PUBLISHERS LTD
61-63 Uxbridge Road, London W5 5SA

TRANSWORLD PUBLISHERS (AUSTRALIA) PTY LTD
15-25 Helles Avenue, Moorebank, NSW 2170

TRANSWORLD PUBLISHERS (NZ) LTD
3 William Pickering Drive, Albany, Auckland

DOUBLEDAY CANADA LTD
105 Bond Street, Toronto, Ontario M5B 1Y3

Published 1995 by Doubleday
a division of Transworld Publishers Ltd

A catalogue record for this book is available
from the British Library

ISBN 0 385 406339

Printed in Belgium by Proost

Over on the Farm

A counting picture book rhyme

Christopher Gunson

DOUBLEDAY

LONDON · NEW YORK · TORONTO · SYDNEY · AUCKLAND

Over on the farm in the early morning sun
lived a clever mother cat
and her little cat one.

'Stretch,' said the mother.
'I stretch,' said the one.

So he stretched and felt warm
in the early morning sun.

Over in the field in the green and the blue
lived a woolly mother sheep
and her little sheep two.

'Leap,' said the mother.
'We leap,' said the two.

So they both leapt together
in the green and the blue.

Over in the pond by an old willow tree
lived a happy mother frog
and her little froggies three.

'Splash,' said the mother.
'We splash,' said the three.

So they splashed and they sploshed
by the old willow tree.

Over in the forest on an oak leaf floor
lived a sly mother fox
and her little foxes four.

'Rustle,' said the mother.
'We rustle,' said the four.

So they rustled and they rolled
on the oak leaf floor.

Over on the hill by a buzzy beehive
lived a fluffy mother rabbit
and her little rabbits five.

'Hop,' said the mother.
'We hop,' said the five.

So they hopped and they jumped
by the buzzy beehive.

Over in the wood in a nest made of sticks
lived a wise mother owl
and her little owls six.

'*Blink*,' said the mother.
'We blink,' said the six.

So they blinked in the sunlight
in the nest made of sticks.

Over in the orchard by a hut old and wooden
lived a fussy mother hen
and her little chicks seven.

'Scratch,' said the mother.
'We scratch,' said the seven.

So they scratched and they pecked
by the hut old and wooden.

Over on the river in the rushes tall and straight
lived a proud mother duck
and her little ducks eight.

'Paddle,' said the mother.
'We paddle,' said the eight.

So they paddled in and out
of the rushes tall and straight.

Over in the garden by a windy washing line
lived a chirpy mother bird
and her little birdies nine.

'Flap,' said the mother.
'We flap,' said the nine.

So they flapped and they cheeped
by the windy washing line.

Over on the farm in a warm muddy pen
lived a kind mother pig
and her little piggies ten.

'*Snuggle*,' said the mother.
'We snuggle,' said the ten.

So they snuggled and they slept
in their warm muddy pen.

one

1

two

2

three

3

four

4

five

5

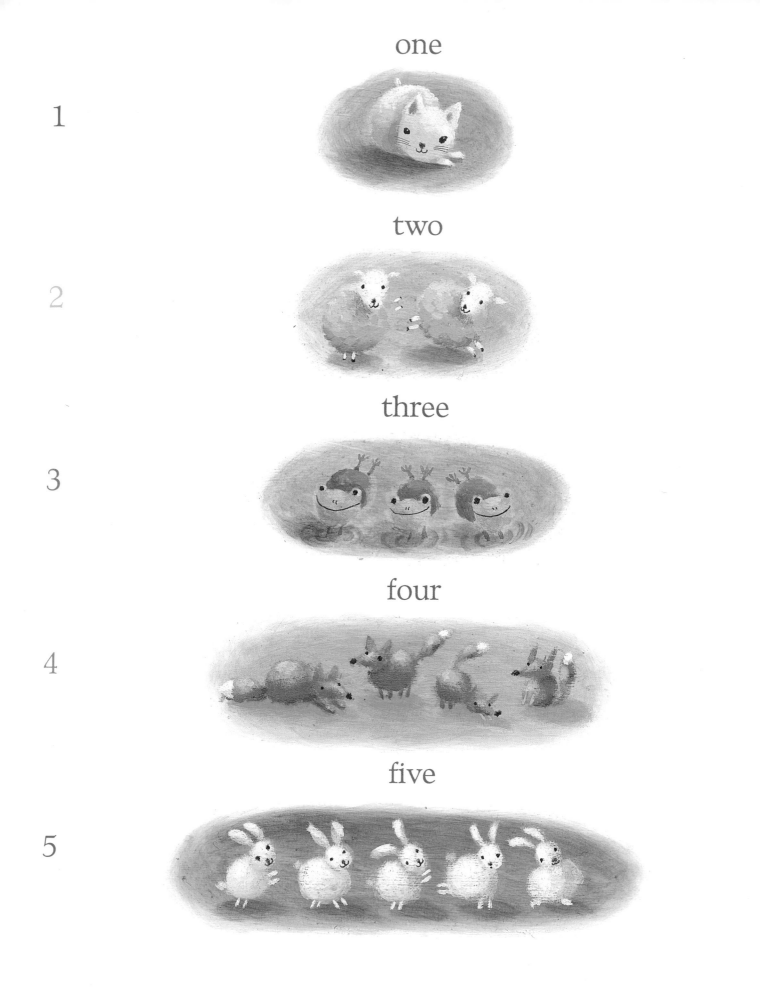

six

6

seven

7

eight

8

nine

9

ten

10

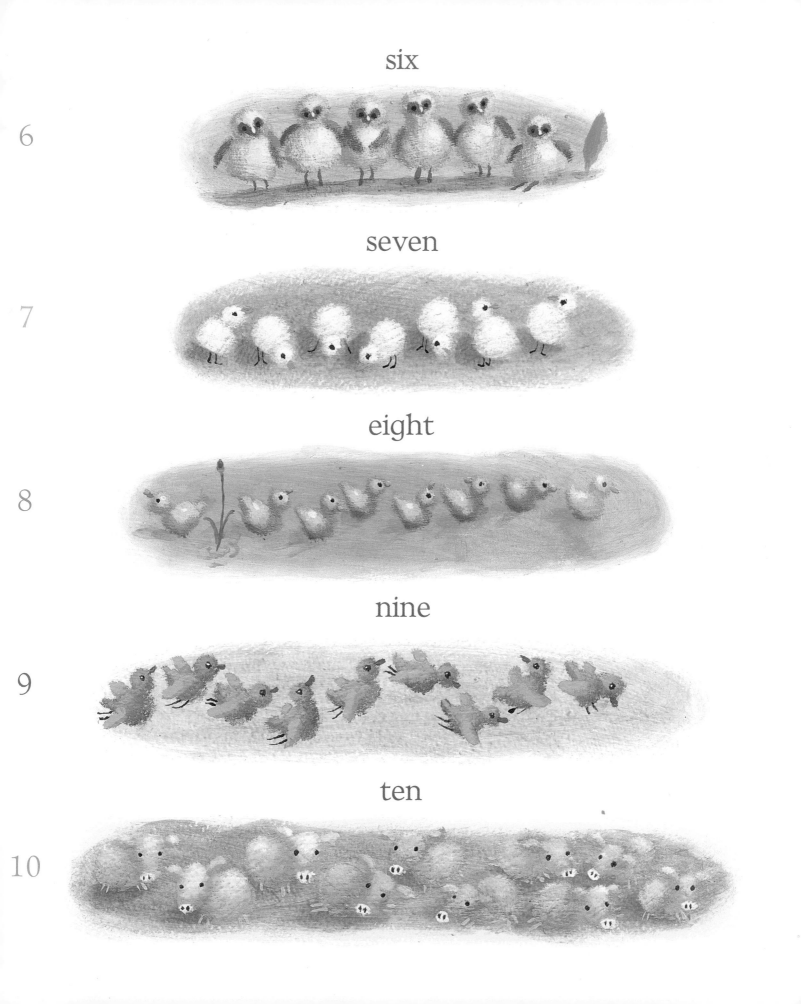